TRIASSIC DINOSAUR WORLD

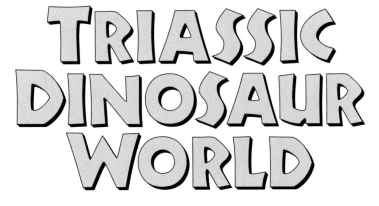

For a free color catalog describing Gareth Stevens' list of high-quality books
and multimedia programs, call 1-800-542-2595 (USA) or 1-800-461-9120
(Canada). Gareth Stevens Publishing's Fax: (414) 225-0377.
See our catalog, too, on the World Wide Web: gsinc.com

Library of Congress Cataloging-in-Publication Data

Green, Tamara, 1945-
    Triassic dinosaur world / by Tamara Green; illustrated by
Richard Grant.
        p. cm. — (World of dinosaurs)
    Includes bibliographical references and index.
    Summary: Takes the reader back 230 million years to the age when
dinosaurs first evolved and describes the world of that time.
    ISBN 0-8368-2175-0 (lib. bdg.)
    1. Dinosaurs—Juvenile literature. 2. Paleontology—Triassic—
Juvenile literature. [1. Dinosaurs. 2. Paleontology.] I. Grant,
Richard, 1959- ill. II. Title. III. Series: World of dinosaurs.
QE862.D5G73487   1998
567.9—dc21   98-8027

This North American edition first published in 1998 by
Gareth Stevens Publishing
1555 North RiverCenter Drive, Suite 201
Milwaukee, Wisconsin 53212 USA

This U.S. edition © 1998 by Gareth Stevens, Inc.
Created with original © 1998 by Quartz Editorial Services,
112 Station Road, Edgware HA8 7AQ U.K.
Additional end matter © 1998 by Gareth Stevens, Inc.

Consultant: Dr. Paul Barrett, Paleontologist, Specialist in Biology and
  Evolution of Dinosaurs, University of Cambridge, England.

Printed in the United States of America

1 2 3 4 5 6 7 8 9 02 01 00 99 98

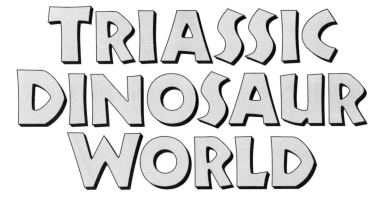

TRIASSIC DINOSAUR WORLD

by Tamara Green
Illustrations by Richard Grant

Gareth Stevens Publishing
MILWAUKEE

CONTENTS

INTRODUCTION

Welcome to the Triassic world of dinosaurs! These amazing animals first appeared on Earth during Triassic times, about 230 million years ago. They flourished and dominated life on our planet for more than 165 million years.

Human beings, of course, had not yet evolved. Nevertheless, through the years, paleontologists have discovered quite a bit about the dinosaurs and their way of life. They have been able to do this work by studying the dinosaurs' fossilized remains.

So what sort of animals were the dinosaurs? Basically, they were reptilian. In a manner that resembled large-scale lizards, they had scaly skin and were egg-layers. Scientists have discovered one important difference between dinosaurs and their modern-day reptilian relatives. Instead of short legs spread-eagled at the sides of their bodies, dinosaurs had legs that were tucked underneath. This helped the huge animals move more quickly.

Dinosaurs, of course, have been extinct for a long time. But it's amazing to think that some of today's animals — crocodiles, for example — lived and thrived at the same time as these prehistoric creatures and still inhabit our planet today. In the first volume of this new, fully illustrated series, we invite you to join us as we dig deep to unearth a fascinating picture of Late Triassic times.

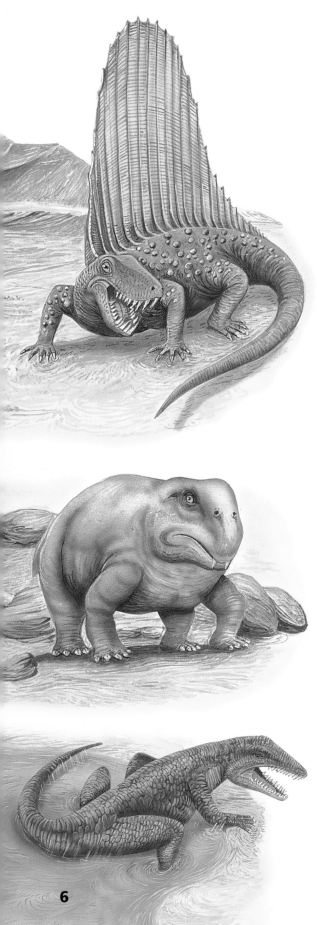

BEFORE THE DINOSAURS

What types of creatures existed on Earth before the dinosaurs appeared in Triassic times? Why did these earlier animals become extinct, allowing the dinosaurs to rule supreme?

Two **Lagosuchus** sparred on a rocky outcrop one steamy Triassic afternoon (*opposite*). These long-legged, rabbit-sized creatures were carnivores; they enjoyed playful fighting when not hunting for small prey.

Missing link?

Unearthed in South America, **Lagosuchus** seems to have been so similar to a dinosaur that paleontologists think it may have been the creature from which dinosaurs evolved. But what was life like on Earth before **Lagosuchus**, during the many millions of years before the age of the dinosaurs, which began about 230 million years ago?

According to some scientists, life on Earth began around 3,500 million years ago as a sort of giant "soup." This "soup" contained simple, single-celled organisms and a type of blue-green algae.

Early vertebrates (animals with backbones) probably originated in the seas; it took a long time before any crawled out of the water. After this happened, however, reptiles and other land animals began to evolve.

Some of the creatures that populated the world before the time of the dinosaurs were extraordinary in appearance. **Dimetrodon** (*left, top*), for example, dates from Permian times, about 270 million years ago. It was a sail-backed reptile about 11 feet (3.3 meters) long. The structure on its back probably helped control body temperature.

Toward the end of Permian times, **Dimetrodon**, together with the majority of species that had evolved by then, seems to have suddenly become extinct. Some scientists speculate this may have occurred because of changes in sea level, while others believe it was due to great changes in climate. A number of experts, however, put the blame on tremendous volcanic eruptions that poured out masses of boiling lava, ash, and poisonous gas.

New species

Evidence exists, however, that some creatures survived, and that entirely new species soon evolved. For example, **Lystrosaurus** (*opposite, center*) was probably a survivor. Fossil remains indicate that this stocky herbivore must have inhabited regions that today include India, South Africa, China, and South America.

    Proterosuchus (*opposite, bottom*), meanwhile, was an early archosaur, a reptile also found worldwide and an ancestor of today's crocodiles.

    We invite you now to turn the page and meet the creature many paleontologists consider to have been the very first dinosaur. It was a small, predatory carnivore and most likely a descendant of **Lagosuchus**. Soon, many other types of dinosaurs would evolve to share the Triassic world.

THE VERY FIRST DINOSAURS

Dinosaurs did not appear on Earth until Late Triassic times. They must have been rare at first; but, over millions of years, their numbers increased, as did their size and variety.

A crafty **Staurikosaurus** that had been lurking in the forest undergrowth suddenly leaped out from behind a tree and snapped its jaws at a passing lizard. Although the lizard had been camouflaged among the fallen leaves and dense bushes, the **Staurikosaurus** had been watching its every move for some time. It would soon provide a tasty meal for the hungry predator.

Successful hunter

Staurikosaurus was among the earliest of the dinosaurs — and possibly the first. At only 6.5 feet (2 m) in length, this carnivore was small by later dinosaur standards. Nevertheless, it was probably a successful predator that also hunted much larger prey at times. It may even have traveled in packs and has been described by some experts as the "first dinosaurian big-game hunter."

Its victims must have included small plant-eating dinosaurs, such as the 3-foot (1-m)-long **Pisanosaurus**, as well as rhynchosaurs — tusked, piglike reptiles that were fairly common in Triassic times. **Staurikosaurus** may have also been a scavenger, feeding on the carcasses, or remains, of any dead rhynchosaurs it encountered.

These lightweight, primitive dinosaurs — estimated to weigh only about 66 pounds (30 kilograms) — had slim yet powerful legs.

They were bipedal and would have been able to run at high speeds when pursuing prey, which they could then clutch in their clawed, five-fingered forelimbs.

Remains of **Staurikosaurus** have been unearthed in South America, mainly in Santa Maria, in southern Brazil.

Frenguellisaurus was much like **Staurikosaurus**, although it was larger. Its remains were found in northwestern Argentina, in South America. It, too, had strong jaws and was an excellent hunter. Many discoveries of very early dinosaurs have been made in South America, where Triassic rocks have become exposed.

Fanged creature

Another bipedal carnivore, **Herrerasaurus**, was also found in Argentina. Scientists discovered a fanglike tooth among its remains.

This tooth probably stuck out from the front of its upper jaw. Its bite must also have been very strong because of the way its lower jaw appears to have been hinged. One snap, and any unfortunate small prey would have found it almost impossible to struggle free.

Several skeletons of 10-foot (3-m)-long **Herrerasaurus** have now been discovered. It was named after the farmer, Victorino Herrera, who first came across this dinosaur by accident.

Most of the world's first dinosaurs were carnivores, hardly bigger than today's large dogs. But within a few million years, both herbivores and carnivores would dominate life on Earth — as they would continue to do for more than 165 million years. Humans have existed for only a tiny fraction of that time and did not evolve until long after the dinosaurs became extinct 65 million years ago.

9

TRIASSIC LANDSCAPES

About 220 million years ago, most of the world's great landmass, known as Pangaea, formed a single supercontinent in the seas. Earth, both from the ground and outer space, would have looked very different from the way it does today.

A young **Procompsognathus** suddenly stopped eating, disturbed by the squawking of pterosaurs overhead. Curious and anxious, it surveyed the landscape as a distant volcano erupted furiously. Such eruptions were common in Triassic times, when Earth was experiencing more changes than it does today. It is not surprising, then, that **Procompsognathus**'s companion did not take much notice. It was hot, and this dinosaur was preoccupied with the joys of splashing in a cool, shallow pool.

Occasional oases

Temperatures in Triassic times probably rarely dropped below 60° Fahrenheit (15° Celsius), even in regions far from the equator. Areas of forest existed alongside huge expanses of arid desert, many with shifting dunes and rocky outcrops. In the deserts, sudden rainstorms would produce the occasional oasis or wadi, as if by magic. Plant-eating dinosaurs could find plenty of available food in these places.

As yet, there was no grass or any flowering plants. Many millions of years would have to pass before these types of vegetation appeared, as paleobotanists (scientists who study the fossilized remains of plant life) discovered. Instead, seed ferns and horsetails flourished in pockets of dense vegetation beside rivers and lakes. Taller vegetation would have included large conifers, groves of cypresses, ginkgoes, and cycads.

New continents

Dinosaurs could wander all over the world's one great super-continent. Toward the end of Triassic times, however, Pangaea (which means "all Earth") began to split into two main areas — Laurasia (comprising what is now North America, Europe, Asia, and the Arctic) and Gondwana (what is now South America, Africa, India, Antarctica, and Australia). Once this began to happen, some types of dinosaurs became more isolated.

EARLY PLANT-EATERS

They were not even close in size to the massive, long-necked sauropods of later Jurassic times, but the majority of Triassic plant-eaters, known as prosauropods, had a similar body shape and eating habits.

A young, hungry **Mussaurus** chomped energetically on a clump of crisp leaves. This was its first meal of the day, and its small, leaf-shaped teeth bit easily into the tough vegetation. However, it was not equipped to chew its breakfast adequately and had to rely on another method to help digest its food.

Swallowing stones

Paleontologists believe many of these early plant-eating dinosaurs swallowed small stones, known as gastroliths, in the same way that Jurassic sauropods such as **Brachiosaurus** were to do millions of years later — and just as some modern birds and reptiles do today. Once inside the dinosaurs' gizzards, these stones would grind up all the vegetation they had consumed, thereby preventing indigestion.

Mussaurus — discovered in what is now Argentina, in South America — grew to an adult size of only 10 feet (3 m) in length. In fact, the smallest dinosaur skeleton ever found — that of a newborn, measuring just 1 foot (30 cm) in length — was a baby **Mussaurus**. It was so small you could have easily held this tiny young herbivore in the palms of your hands.

Riojasaurus, also from Argentina, was slightly larger and heavier than **Mussaurus**.

Plant-eating **Nyasasaurus**, another prosauropod found near Lake Nyasa in what is now Tanzania, Africa, was smaller — just 7 feet (2.1 m) in length. About the same size was the most primitive prosauropod discovered so far, found in what is now England. Like all the other prosauropods, it had a small head, and a long neck and tail. It had short arms with big thumb claws. Two of its remaining four fingers were small and clawless. Its name, **Thecodontosaurus**, means "socket-toothed lizard;" and it was a prosauropod, even though its name suggests it may have been a thecodont (a relative of the dinosaurs).

Even the largest prosauropods — including 26-foot (8-m)-long **Plateosaurus** among them — may have had to rear up on their hind legs to feed on high-growing vegetation at times.

Not all Triassic herbivores were prosauropods, however. Tiny 3-foot (1-m)-long **Pisanosaurus,** from Argentina, for example, was the earliest-known ornithischian (a group of dinosaurs that had birdlike hips). Thick-necked, bipedal **Technosaurus** — discovered in Texas, in the United States — was also among the Triassic plant-eaters but, again, it was not a prosauropod. **Technosaurus** measured about 13 feet (4 m) in length and had leaflike teeth.

Huge appetites

All these herbivores — even the tiniest — would have consumed huge amounts of vegetation. Their droppings would have been considerable, fertilizing the ground so that further abundant vegetation flourished. These herbivores were constantly in danger, since predatory, carnivorous dinosaurs had healthy appetites. The carnivores' diet included not only meals of smaller creatures such as lizards, but also other dinosaurs, as you will soon discover.

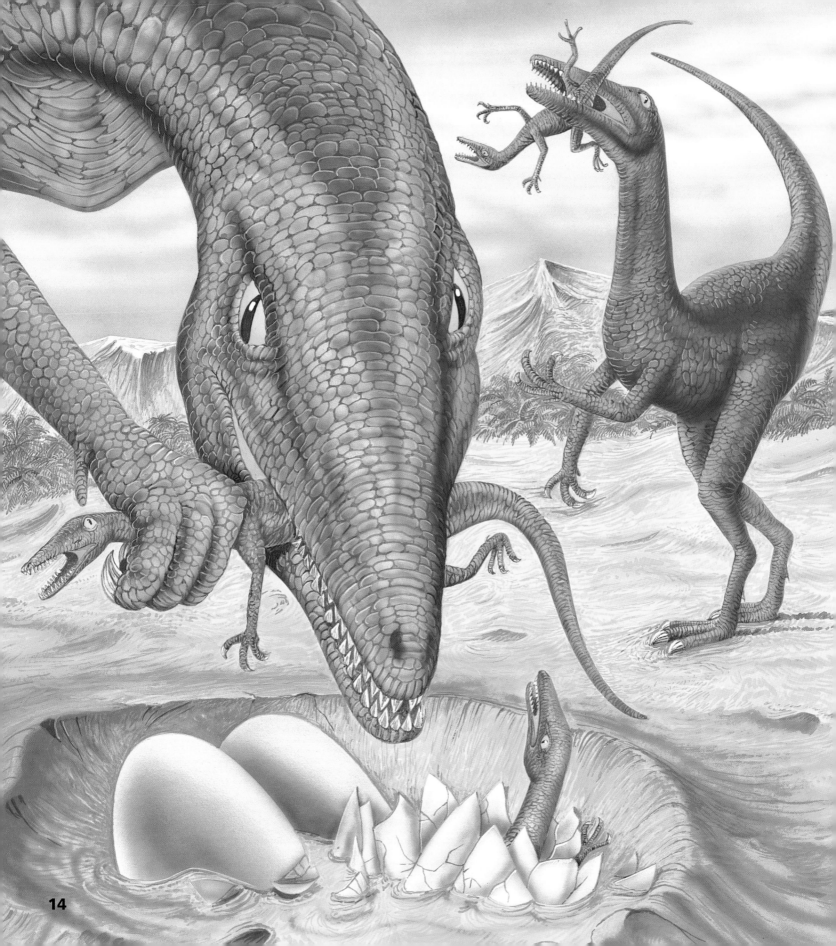

EARLY CARNIVORES

Many of the very first dinosaurs were meat-eaters, and some, it seems, may even have been cannibals. Scientists have found compelling evidence of this — at Ghost Ranch!

The hungry adult **Coelophysis** held the struggling baby in its mouth. The newborn dinosaur had just hatched from the comfort and warmth of a large egg, and had been trying to find its way out of the nest by scrambling over pieces of broken shell. Now the frightened baby cried out as one of its parents grasped its fragile body and took a bite with its many-toothed jaws.

Another newborn, meanwhile, was just emerging from an egg and looked around nervously. Would it share the same fate — like a third member of the clutch, already being gulped down by another adult in the pack?

Coelophysis, whose name means "hollow form," was among the very first dinosaurs to evolve on Earth. This carnivore was first described in 1889 by the highly respected paleontologist, Edward Drinker Cope. Not until 1947, however, did paleontologists have a very good picture of this dinosaur and its behavior. This new information followed the discovery of an entire graveyard of the species — over one hundred skeletons, in fact — at a site in New Mexico known as Ghost Ranch. Here, the scientists found a remarkable treasure-trove of **Coelophysis** skeletons all huddled together.

Cannibals!

It was quite a find. But most fascinating of all were the skeletons of several tiny baby **Coelophysis** that were discovered in the body cavities of some of the adults. It seemed **Coelophysis** must have resorted to cannibalism at times, either as a regular way of eating or perhaps only when food was in short supply.

From its skeletal remains, we know that **Coelophysis** had a slim body about 10 feet (3 m) long, most of it made up of neck and tail. It weighed only about 65 pounds (30 kg) and had sharp, backward-pointing teeth that enabled it to tear at its prey — including its own young — with ease.

No one knows for sure if other carnivores in Triassic times ate their own young, or whether **Coelophysis** was unique in this respect. Future discoveries of the skeletal remains of other early dinosaurs may, in time, provide such evidence.

What we do know, however, is that most carnivores of Triassic times were nowhere near the size of later dinosaurs, such as **Tyrannosaurus rex**. The Triassic meat-eaters were small in comparison, but potential prey were equally frightened by the Triassic carnivores. However, few remains have been found from Triassic times, probably because the bones of these smaller dinosaurs disintegrated more easily than those of the more gigantic dinosaurs that succeeded them through the millennia.

Plateosaurus

Remains of plant-eating **Plateosaurus** (PLAT-EE-OH-<u>SAW</u>-RUS) have been dug up in western Europe. It grew to about 26 feet (8 m) long and could rear up on its hind legs to feed.

Pisanosaurus

The earliest ornithischian discovered so far, **Pisanosaurus** (PEA-<u>SAHN</u>-OH-<u>SAW</u>-RUS) was native to Argentina. This tiny, bipedal herbivore grew to only 3 feet (1 m) in length.

Syntarsus

Bipedal, carnivorous **Syntarsus** (SIN-<u>TAR</u>-SUS) was 10 feet (3 m) in length and had long, narrow jaws. Its fossilized bones have been found in both Zimbabwe, in Africa, and Arizona, in the United States.

Procompsognathus

Procompsognathus (PRO-<u>COMP</u>-SOG-<u>NAY</u>-THOOS), a small carnivore only 4 feet (1.2 m) long, lived in what is now Germany. Two of the five fingers on this theropod's hands were shorter than the others.

GALLERY-1

Mussaurus

Plant-eating **Mussaurus**
(MUSS-OR-RUS), from Argentina,
grew from the tiniest of hatchlings
to about 10 feet (3 m) in length.
It could walk on four legs or two,
and had a long, strong, tail.

Saltopus

Found in Scotland, **Saltopus**
(SALT-OH-PUS), a miniature
bipedal carnivore just 2 feet
(60 cm) in length, was no bigger
than a goose and weighed
only 2 pounds (900 g).

Coelophysis

First discovered in the U.S., **Coelophysis** (SEEL-OH-<u>FEYE</u>-SIS) was a small, bipedal, sharp-toothed carnivore believed to have been cannibalistic at times. It grew up to 10 feet (3 m) in length and weighed 60 pounds (27 kg) at most because of its hollow bones.

Revueltosaurus

Revueltosaurus (RAY-VOO-<u>ELT</u>-OH-<u>SAW</u>-RUS), from New Mexico, was a bipedal plant-eater with a thick neck. From its snout to the tip of its tail, it was about 3 feet (1 m) long.

Likhoelosaurus

The large prosauropod **Likhoelosaurus** (LIK-HO-<u>EL</u>-OH-<u>SAW</u>-RUS) was discovered in Lesotho, in Africa. This four-legged herbivore measured about 13 feet (4 m) in length.

GALLERY-2

Ischisaurus

Among the very first dinosaurs, **Ischisaurus** (ISK-EE-SAW-RUS) was a bipedal carnivore that was unearthed in Argentina. It was only about 6.5 feet (2 m) long, but still a fierce predator.

Sellosaurus

Lightly built and four-legged, **Sellosaurus** (SELL-OH-SAW-RUS) was a 33-foot (10-m)-long herbivore. It had five-fingered forelimbs with large thumb claws and roamed what is now Germany.

Melanosaurus

A large South African prosauropod with a small head, **Melanosaurus** (MEL-AN-OH-SAW-RUS) had a bulky body and legs like an elephant's. Its tail made up much of its 40-foot (12-m) body length.

TRIASSIC

Herrerasaurus

Another bipedal meat-eater and one of the earliest-known dinosaurs, **Herrerasaurus** (HAIR-AIR-AH-SAW-RUS), from Argentina, was 10 feet (3 m) long and had sharp teeth.

Coloradisaurus

Found in Argentina, the plant-eating prosauropod **Coloradisaurus** (CAHL-O-RAH-DEE-SAW-RUS) was about 13 feet (4 m) in length. It could move around on all four limbs and rear up on its hind legs to reach into the treetops.

Riojasaurus

Also from Argentina, **Riojasaurus** (REE-OH-HA-SAW-RUS) was a 36-foot (11-m)-long quadruped. A prosauropod, it had a small head, a bulky body, and a long neck and tail.

GALLERY-3

Halticosaurus

With a name meaning "nimble lizard," **Halticosaurus** (HAL-TIK-OH-<u>SAW</u>-RUS) lived in western Europe. A bipedal carnivore about 18 feet (5.5 m) in length, it had strong jaws and slim legs.

Aliwalia

From South Africa, **Aliwalia** (AL-EE-<u>WAHL</u>-EE-AH) was about 25 feet (nearly 8 m) long. Weighing as much as 1.5 tons, it was one of the heaviest early carnivores.

Staurikosaurus

Staurikosaurus (STOW-RIK-OH-<u>SAW</u>-RUS), a very primitive dinosaur found in Brazil, was a bipedal, sharp-toothed carnivore only 6.5 feet (2 m) long.

THE TRIASSIC DAY

As this aerial view shows, Plateosaurus, one of the best-known dinosaurs from Triassic times, lived in herds. How did they pass their time, and what dangers did they face?

A mother **Plateosaurus** nuzzled one of her young. It was vital to coax the baby dinosaur into the center of the herd so the adults could protect it from the attacks of predators.

On the run

But the adults, too, had to be constantly on guard. At any time, a hungry carnivore might appear — worse still, a pack of them. Then it would be time for the herd, including the babies, to run for their lives.

But there were other dangers, too, that a herd of **Plateosaurus** might have had to face in the course of a Triassic day. At times, these typical prosauropods must have almost wilted in the heat of the midday sun. They probably would have sought a cool drink from a nearby river or pool, perhaps also venturing to take a refreshing dip in the water in order to cool down.

It is unlikely that dinosaurs would have been able to swim. However, it is possible they might have paddled through the water in an attempt to reduce their body temperature.

Stuck in the mud

Some waterways, however, must have been extremely muddy, and it is possible that many paddling dinosaurs became stuck in the silt. In fact, at times, a whole herd may have become trapped together, sinking into the prehistoric mire. Their forelimbs had large thumb claws — useful to some extent when grappling with an enemy, but of no benefit at all when trying to haul themselves out of muddy waters.

That, at least, is what some paleontologists believe as a result of the discovery of a whole herd of **Plateosaurus** skeletons at Trossingen, Germany, in 1921. Nine complete dinosaurs were unearthed there, together with many more partial skeletons and bone fragments.

Intriguingly, many of the skeletons were found with their abdomens downward rather than lying on their sides — a sign that they may have perished while standing up in mud. Some experts, however, think it is more likely that the **Plateosaurus** died together somewhere else, and that their bodies washed up on the sand banks. Others, meanwhile, favor the theory that the dinosaurs died together in one spot as the result of a sandstorm.

Friedrich von Huene, one of the paleontologists who studied **Plateosaurus** in great detail, believed that there were two main seasons in Triassic times: one wet, and the other dry. During the wet season, herds of **Plateosaurus** would wander in the wooded hills where food was plentiful. When there were storms, some dinosaurs may have become separated from the rest of the herd because of sudden flash-flooding, as shown in this illustration (*right, top*).

During the dry season, herds of **Plateosaurus** would head for lakes and rivers in search of new water sources and food supplies. The carnivorous dinosaurs probably followed, constantly on the trail of the plant-eaters that were a prime source of nourishment for these meat-eaters.

Volcanoes were also a common feature of Triassic times. The peace of a prehistoric afternoon frequently may have been shattered by sudden volcanic eruptions. Any dinosaurs unfortunate enough to be caught in the path of the resulting boiling lava flow certainly would have died.

Feeding was undoubtedly the main preoccupation of the dinosaurs; they would have spent most of their waking hours fulfilling their dietary needs. It is unlikely that the prosauropods were active mainly at night, or nocturnal. After darkness had descended, they would have rested, keeping together in case predators chose the twilight hours to make a sudden attack.

Large Triassic marine reptiles were able to swim as well as any fish, but they needed to come up for air at intervals.

The open-jawed marine creature (*above*) looked on as a larger sea-going reptile prepared to eat the first of many fish it would devour that prehistoric day. Out of the water, **Nothosaurus** — remains of which have been found in many parts of the globe — could probably only amble along like a seal. At times, however, as in this scene, it went ashore to sleep in the sun on a clifftop or to lay the eggs that produced its young.

Some marine reptiles had much longer necks, however. **Tanystrophaeus**, for instance — with a name meaning "long,

twisted neck" — had a very slim, snakelike neck that was much longer than the rest of its body. Experts have suggested that it may have used its neck like a fishing rod, remaining on dry land or in shallow water to dip its built-in rod into the sea, and then spearing passing fish with its small, sharp-toothed jaws.

Fantastic flippers

Pistosaurus (*opposite*) also had a fairly long but somewhat sturdier neck. It had developed strong flippers, too, that would have turned it into an extremely

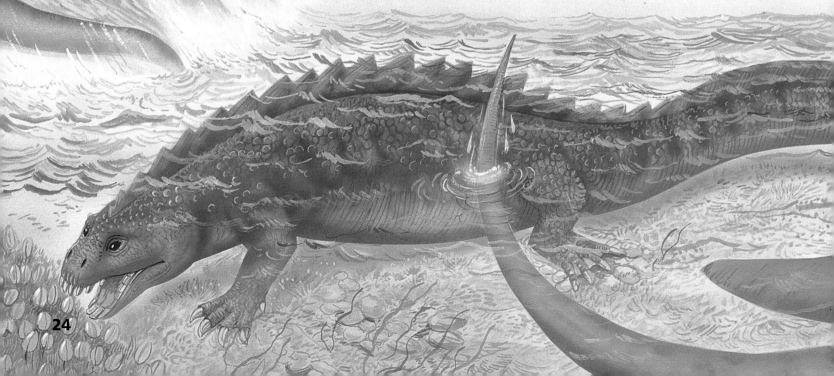

good swimmer. It probably ventured much farther out to sea than other less-evolved Triassic marine reptiles. **Pistosaurus** also seemed to resemble the fabled Loch Ness Monster, an enormous creature said to lurk today in one of Scotland's many beautiful lakes, called lochs.

Crushing teeth

Dolphinlike ichthyosaurs, which grew to 50 feet (15 m) in length, also hunted fish and crustaceans in Triassic times. **Placodus** (*center*) searched for food in the water, but this 8-foot (2.5-m)-long animal lived mainly on land. Short-necked, with a long tail and an armored body, it had strong, blunt teeth that were ideal for crushing open the casings of mollusks and other shellfish. In fact, all the large marine creatures would have fed from the small sea life of the warm Triassic waters.

IN THE TRIASSIC SEAS

IN THE TRIASSIC SKIES

While various species of Triassic dinosaurs began to evolve on Earth, many different flying reptiles — known as pterosaurs — took to the air.

A group of winged creatures, all hungry for a meal of seafood, swooped down to the ocean's edge. Diving to the surface, they grabbed unsuspecting fish and quickly gobbled down their feast. They were masters of the prehistoric skies but are now long extinct. How, then, was the pterosaur first discovered?

When paleontologist Mario Pandolfi first unearthed the remains of a pterosaur in Italy in 1973, its winged fingers were missing, as were most of its hind legs. Nevertheless, he immediately recognized it as a pterosaur.

This discovery was very exciting. The rock in which it had become fossilized could be accurately dated to Late Triassic times. The flying reptile was therefore about 200 million years old!

Named **Eudimorphodon**, it had a wingspan of about 3 feet (1 m), a long tail, and sharp teeth that were ideal for catching slithery fish. In fact, Pandolfi actually found some fish bones among its fossilized stomach contents.

Until they were full-grown, however, these pterosaurs probably had teeth more suited to catching insects, such as dragonflies, as shown (*opposite, far right*) in this illustration.

Fish-lovers

More recently, in 1978, another smaller pterosaur, **Peteinosaurus** (*center*), was unearthed nearby.

Given a name that means, quite literally, "winged reptile," it had a wingspan reaching just 2 feet (60 cm). Although not enormous, it must still have looked fairly impressive as it swooped down to the water.

Preondactylus (*left*) was the oldest pterosaur of all and was even smaller. Its remains were found tightly

packed together, an indication
that it may have been the prey of
another prehistoric creature —
one that had coughed up the
pterosaur's undigested bones,
like owl pellets today.

Pterosaurs were accomplished
fliers, yet they were entirely
unrelated to birds. In fact, many
millions of years passed before
birds evolved from the dinosaurs
and began to fly with the
pterosaurs — the largest
winged creatures that
ever existed.

OTHER TRIASSIC CREATURES

Not only dinosaurs first appeared on Earth in Late Triassic times. Several new forms of animal life emerged alongside the dinosaurs — including crocodiles, frogs, turtles, large seagoing reptiles, pterosaurs, and the earliest mammals.

A heavily armored young **Desmatosuchus** (*left, top*) snapped its snout, but a nearby frog resting on a rock did not move. Instinctively, it knew that it did not need to rush away. In time, this snapping aetosaur might grow to some 16 feet (5 m) in length; but, as a plant-eater, or herbivore, it would not harm the frog. Instead, it would choose to uplift plants, tubers, and roots with its specially adapted jaws.

Aetosaurs (the name means "old lizards") had small, leaf-shaped teeth and were related to the dinosaurs. These four-legged reptiles were, in fact, the only plant-eating thecodonts — reptiles that finally became extinct by the end of the Triassic era when dinosaurs began to rule.

On the alert

Alongside these peaceful aetosaurs, however, lived predatory thecodonts that were even more crocodilelike and which frogs would have had to avoid in the daily fight for survival. Small amphibians such as these had to be always on the alert since several of the thecodonts were land-dwellers, or terrestrial, rather than water-dwellers, or aquatic; and some may even have hunted in packs. Peaceful turtles, too — which were common by Late Triassic times — may have provided the thecodonts with sumptuous feasts.

Extraordinary, and possibly colorful, lizards — such as **Icarosaurus**, shown here — would have been another common feature of the Late Triassic landscape. They could not fly like the pterosaurs. However, a membrane that was stretched over their ribs served as a type of parachute that enabled them to glide elegantly and easily between branches.

The warm climate in these Triassic times would also have been ideal for many types of exotic insects, spiders, and snails — small creatures that provided food for the very first mammals. These early mammals were tiny, shrewlike creatures that probably only dared to venture out in the dark stillness of night, when much larger animals were resting. The risk of falling prey to the meat-eating thecodonts — and, of course, early carnivorous dinosaurs — was always present.

29

GLOSSARY

aetosaurs — the only plant-eating thecodonts, which had small leaf-shaped teeth.

archosaurs — reptiles, including crocodiles, thecodonts, and dinosaurs.

bipedal — related to an animal that has two legs; able to move around on two legs.

camouflaged — colored or shaped in a way that blends in with the background.

cannibals — creatures that eat their own kind.

carcass — the body of a dead animal.

carnivore — a meat-eater.

Cretaceous times — the final era of the dinosaurs, lasting from 144-65 million years ago.

fossilized — embedded and preserved in rocks, resin, or some other material.

gastrolith — one of the numerous small stones swallowed by plant-eating dinosaurs to help with the digestion of tough plant material.

Gondwana — once a segment of the supercontinent, Pangaea. Gondwana included all of the present southern continents.

herbivore — a plant-eater.

ichthyosaurs — extinct marine reptiles that had fishlike bodies and long snouts.

Jurassic times — the middle era of the dinosaurs, lasting from 213-144 million years ago.

Laurasia — once a segment of the supercontinent, Pangaea. Laurasia included all of the present northern continents.

oases — green areas with vegetation and water found within deserts.

originated — came into being; created; started.

ornithischian — a member of a group of dinosaurs that had birdlike hips.

paleobotanist — a scientist who studies the fossilized remains of plants.

paleontologist — a scientist who studies past geologic periods as known from fossil remains.

Pangaea — a supercontinent once comprising all the world's land.

Permian times — the era prior to Triassic times, at the end of which most of Earth's creatures became extinct and which lasted from 290-249 million years ago.

prosauropods — moderately long-necked dinosaurs, all herbivores, principally from Triassic times.

pterosaurs — members of a group of extinct flying reptiles.

rhynchosaurs — piglike reptiles common in Triassic times.

sauropods — long-necked plant-eating dinosaurs primarily from Jurassic times.

scavenge — to eat the leftovers or carcasses of other animals.

speculate — to assume something is true based on a limited amount of evidence.

thecodonts — not dinosaurs, but quadrupedal reptiles from Permian and Triassic times.

Triassic times — the first era of the dinosaurs, lasting from 249 to 213 million years ago.

undergrowth — the bushes and smaller plants that grow under large trees in a forest.

vertebrate — an animal with a backbone.

wadi — a shallow, sharply defined depression in a desert; the bed or valley of a stream that is usually dry except during the rainy season.

MORE BOOKS TO READ

Death from Space: What Killed the Dinosaurs? Isaac Asimov's New Library of the Universe (series). Isaac Asimov and Greg Walz-Chojnacki (Gareth Stevens)

Dinosaurs. Neil Clark (Dorling Kindersley)

Dinosaurs. Claude Delafosse (Scholastic)

Dinosaurs and How They Lived. Steve Parker (Dorling Kindersley)

Draw, Model, and Paint (series): Dinosaurs (3 of 6 vols.). Isidro Sanchez (Gareth Stevens)

Looking at Coelophysis: A Dinosaur from the Triassic Period. Graham Coleman (Gareth Stevens)

Looking at Mussaurus: A Dinosaur from the Triassic Period. Tamara Green (Gareth Stevens)

Looking at Procompsognathus: A Dinosaur from the Triassic Period. Tamara Green (Gareth Stevens)

The New Dinosaur Collection (series). (Gareth Stevens)

The Usborne Book of Dinosaurs. Susan Mayes (Usborne)

VIDEOS

All About Dinosaurs. (United Learning)

Did Comets Kill The Dinosaurs? (Gareth Stevens)

Digging Up Dinosaurs. (Great Plains National Instructional Television Library)

Dinosaur! (series). (Arts & Entertainment Network)

Dinosaurs, Dinosaurs, Dinosaurs. (Twin Tower Enterprises)

Dinosaurs: Remains to Be Seen. (Public Media, Inc.)

Dinosaurs: The Terrible Lizards. (AIMS Media)

WEB SITES

pubs.usgs.gov/gip/dinosaurs

www.enchantedlearning.com/subjects/dinosaurs

www.fmnh.org/exhibits/dino/Triassic.htm

www.dinosociety.org

www.ucmp.berkeley.edu/

www.dinofest.org/links/links

Due to the dynamic nature of the internet, some web sites stay current longer than others. To find additional web sites, use a reliable search engine with one or more of the following keywords to help you locate more information about dinosaurs. Keywords: *dinosaurs, fossils, Jurassic, paleontology, prehistoric, Triassic.*

INDEX